# Colorful Clock

hour hand — — minute hand

— face

Write the **clock numbers**.
Color the **hour hand** blue.
Color the **minute hand** red.
Color the **face** yellow.

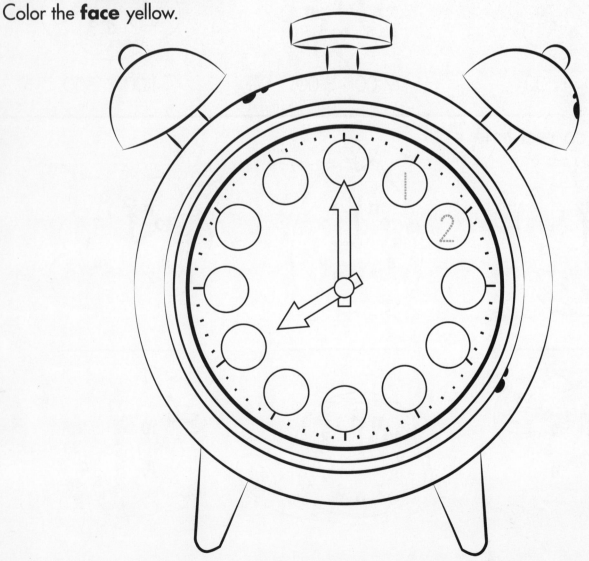

# To the Hour

Circle the correct time.

2:00    1:00

4:00    5:00

8:00    9:00

11:00    12:00

7:00    8:00

1:00    2:00

Write the correct time.

_____

_____

_____

_____

_____

_____

# What Time Is It?

Draw the hour hand on each clock to show the correct time.

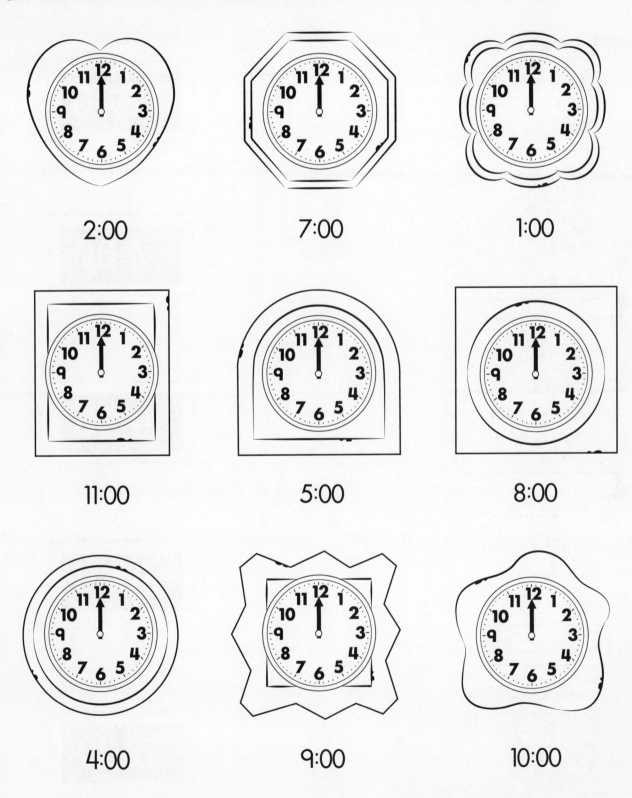

2:00

7:00

1:00

11:00

5:00

8:00

4:00

9:00

10:00

# Matching Clocks

Match the clocks that show the same time.

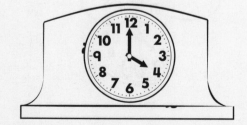 

Telling time to the hour; matching analog and digital clocks

# To the Half Hour

Circle the correct time.

2:30   3:30

5:30   6:30

10:30   10:00

11:30   1:30

9:30   8:30

2:30   2:00

Write the correct time.

_____

_____

_____

_____

_____

_____

# More Clocks to Match

Match the clocks that show the same time.

6:30

1:30

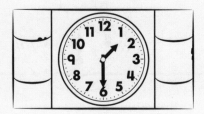 

8:30

11:30

9:30

Telling time to the half hour; matching analog and digital clocks

# Writing Time Two Ways

**8:00**
**or**
**eight o'clock**

Time can be written two ways.

**8:30**
**or**
**half past eight**

## Write the time two ways.

9:00

nine o'clock

_____

_____

_____

_____

_____

_____

_____

_____

_____

_____

# To the Quarter Hour

Circle the correct time.

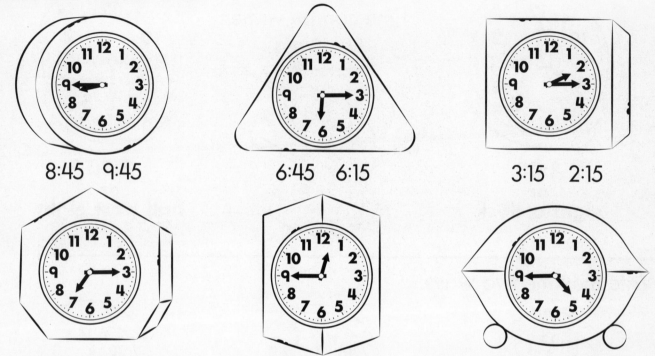

8:45   9:45

6:45   6:15

3:15   2:15

6:15   7:15

12:45   12:15

4:45   3:45

Write the correct time.

Telling time to the quarter hour

# Make a Match

Match the clocks that show the same time.

7:45

9:15

10:45

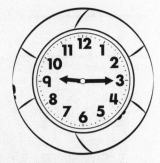

6:15

2:15

# You Can Say That Again

It is 7:15.

It is a quarter after seven.

---

Write the time two ways.

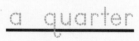
5:45

a quarter

to six

_____

_____

_____

_____

_____

_____

_____

_____

_____

_____

_____

_____

_____

_____

_____

Writing time to the quarter hour two ways

# Now and Later

Fill in the ○ to show the time one hour later.

○ 9:15
○ 10:15

○ 11:30
○ 12:30

○ 3:00
○ 3:30

○ 6:15
○ 7:15

○ 3:30
○ 3:45

○ 2:00
○ 2:30

○ 9:00
○ 9:15

○ 9:30
○ 8:30

○ 3:00
○ 5:00

# In an Hour

Draw the time one hour later.

| NOW | LATER | NOW | LATER |
|---|---|---|---|
|  |  |  |  |

| NOW | LATER | NOW | LATER |
|---|---|---|---|
|  |  |  | 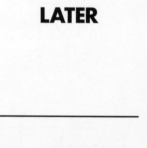 |

Write the time one hour later.

| NOW | LATER | NOW | LATER |
|---|---|---|---|
|  | _____ |  | _____ |

| NOW | LATER | NOW | LATER |
|---|---|---|---|
|  | _____ |  | _____ |

Showing time one hour later

# Five at a Time

There are 60 minutes in an hour.
Each number on a clock represents 5 minutes.

Count by 5's to write the 5-minute intervals around the clock.

# Time for Fives

Circle the correct time.

3:25   3:35

6:40   6:30

11:20   10:20

1:30   1:05

9:55   10:55

2:30   2:40

Write the correct time.

_____

_____

_____

_____

_____

_____

Telling time in 5-minute intervals

# Watch the Time

Match the clocks that show the same time.

Telling time in 5-minute intervals; matching analog and digital clocks

# Same Time

Match each clock with the correct time.

twenty-five minutes after three

thirty-five minutes after eleven

five minutes after eight

fifty minutes after five

twenty minutes after twelve

ten minutes after six

Showing time in 5-minute intervals

# One at a Time

Each hour is made up of 60 minutes.
The 60 minutes go around a clock.

Count by 1's to write the minutes around the clock.

# To the Minute

Circle the correct time.

8:02   8:07            5:58   6:02            2:17   2:13

3:18   3:28            7:32   7:37            4:46   4:09

Write the correct time.

_____            _____            _____

_____            _____            _____

Telling time to the minute

# Minute Match

Match the clocks that show the same time.

# One to One

Match each clock with the correct time.

twenty-seven minutes after one

eleven minutes after five

twenty-one minutes after six

nineteen minutes after two

thirty-seven minutes after five

# Do You Have the Time?

Draw the hour and minute hand on each clock to show the correct time.

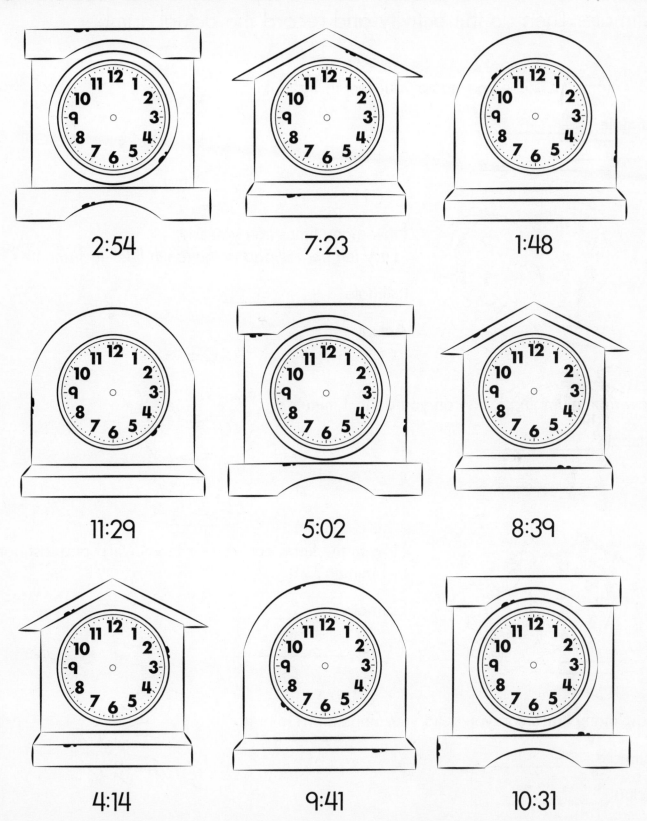

2:54          7:23          1:48

11:29          5:02          8:39

4:14          9:41          10:31

# Got a Minute?

How many times can you do each activity in a minute? First estimate. Then do the activity and record the actual number.

How many times can you stomp your feet in 1 minute?

Estimate _____

Actual _____

How many times can you say, "Lucy left her lollipop in the lunch line" in 1 minute?

Estimate _____

Actual _____

How many jumping jacks can you do in 1 minute?

Estimate _____

Actual _____

How many times can you write your first and last name in 1 minute?

Estimate _____

Actual _____

How many times can you snap your fingers in 1 minute?

Estimate _____

Actual _____

Understanding the length of a minute

# Passing Time

Elapsed time is used to find out how much time has passed. If you start playing a game at 3:00 and finish at 3:30, the elapsed time is 30 minutes or a half hour.

Read both clocks. Write how much time has elapsed.

**START**      **STOP**

Elapsed Time: _____

**START**      **STOP**

Elapsed Time: _____

**START**      **STOP**

Elapsed Time: _____

**START**      **STOP**

Elapsed Time: _____

**START**      **STOP**

6:45      7:00

Elapsed Time: _____

**START**      **STOP**

1:15      2:15

Elapsed Time: _____

**START**      **STOP**

3:10      3:40

Elapsed Time: _____

**START**      **STOP**

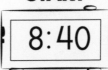

8:40      3:45

Elapsed Time: _____

# How Much Time Elapsed?

Read each problem and solve.

Lisa's bus picked her up at 8:00. She got to school at 8:15. How long was she on the bus?

start time _____

finish time _____

elapsed time _____

Mary's math class started at 10:30 and ended at 11:15. How long was the class?

start time _____

finish time _____

elapsed time _____

Tommy went to lunch at 12:00 and then to recess at 12:30. How long was lunchtime?

start time _____

finish time _____

elapsed time _____

Fred started writing a story at 2:00 and finished at 2:25. How long did it take him to write his story?

start time _____

finish time _____

elapsed time _____

Aaron had a snack after school at 4:10. He started his homework 15 minutes later. What time did Aaron start his homework?

start time _____

finish time _____

elapsed time _____

Rosemary and her mom went to the store at 6:00. They were gone for one hour. What time did they get home?

start time _____

finish time _____

elapsed time _____

Curtis practiced the piano at 7:30. He practiced three songs in twenty minutes. What time was Curtis finished practicing?

start time _____

finish time _____

elapsed time _____

Laura likes to read before she goes to sleep. She started reading at 8:00 and read for 30 minutes. What time did Laura stop reading?

start time _____

finish time _____

elapsed time _____

*Solving word problems with elapsed time*

# Practice Sessions

| Sport | Begins | Ends |
|---|---|---|
| Baseball | 6:00 | 8:00 |
| Football | 4:30 | 5:30 |
| Swimming | 5:15 | 6:15 |
| Soccer | 4:00 | 6:00 |

Use the schedule to answer the questions.

1. Which practice begins at a quarter after five? _____

2. How long does the baseball practice last? _____

3. Which practice starts 30 minutes after soccer? _____

4. Which practices are two hours long? _____

5. Which practice ends the latest? _____

# Things To Do

| | visit grandparents | go to grocery store | get haircut |
|---|---|---|---|
| 2 hours | ■ | | |
| 1 hours and 30 minutes | ■ | ■ | |
| 1 hour | ■ | ■ | ■ |
| 30 minutes | ■ | ■ | ■ |

Use the graph to answer the questions.

1. Which activity will take the least amount of time?

_____

2. Which will take the most amount of time?

_____

3. How much longer is the trip to the grocery store than getting a haircut?

_____

4. How long will it take to do all three activities?

_____

5. Name another activity that takes about the same amount of time as getting your haircut.

_____

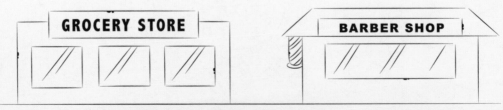

Using a graph to solve time problems

# Calendar Time

## JUNE

| Sun | Mon | Tues | Wed | Thurs | Fri | Sat |
|-----|-----|------|-----|-------|-----|-----|
| 1   | 2   | 3    | 4   | 5     | 6   | 7   |
| 8   | 9   | 10   | 11  | 12    | 13  | 14  |
| 15  | 16  | 17   | 18  | 19    | 20  | 21  |
| 22  | 23  | 24   | 25  | 26    | 27  | 28  |
| 29  | 30  |      |     |       |     |     |

Use the calendar to answer the questions.

1. What is the first day of the week? _____

2. How many days are in one week? _____

3. How many Mondays are in this month? _____

4. What day of the week is June 27? _____

5. Write the date that is five days after June 6. _____

6. What date will it be one week after June 19? _____

7. What is the last day of this month? _____

# Coins

1 penny = 1¢

1 nickel = 5¢

1 dime = 10¢

1 quarter = 25¢

## Count by 1's to add the pennies.

Total Amount

1 2 _____ _____ _____ _____ _____ ¢

## Count by 5's to add the nickels.

Total Amount

_____ _____ _____ _____ _____ ¢

## Count by 10's to add the dimes.

Total Amount

_____ _____ _____ _____ _____ _____ _____ _____ ¢

## Count by 25's to add the quarters.

Total Amount

_____ _____ _____ ¢

Understanding the value of coins

# Coin Match

Match the coins to the correct amount.

35¢

42¢

78¢

13¢

81¢

94¢

39¢

67¢

# More or Less?

Count the coins. Then write >, <, or = to compare the amounts.

---

Write >, <, or = to compare the amounts.

| | | | | | | | |
|---|---|---|---|---|---|---|---|
| 74¢ ☐ 47¢ | 91¢ ☐ 61¢ | 25¢ ☐ 25¢ | 41¢ ☐ 14¢ |
| 19¢ ☐ 29¢ | 20¢ ☐ 70¢ | 31¢ ☐ 13¢ | 51¢ ☐ 51¢ |
| 21¢ ☐ 12¢ | 83¢ ☐ 88¢ | 69¢ ☐ 96¢ | 37¢ ☐ 53¢ |
| 34¢ ☐ 40¢ | 70¢ ☐ 17¢ | 45¢ ☐ 45¢ | 11¢ ☐ 1¢ |

Comparing coin values and amounts

# Counting Coins

Count the coins. Write the total amount.

Total _____ ¢

Total _____ ¢

Total _____ ¢

Total _____ ¢

Total _____ ¢

# Counting Big to Small

Counting money is easiest when you start with the largest amount.

First count the quarters.

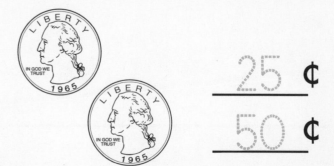

25 ¢

50 ¢

Next add the dimes.

_____ ¢

_____ ¢

_____ ¢

_____ ¢

Then add the nickels.

_____ ¢

Finally add the pennies.

_____ ¢

_____ ¢

_____ ¢

_____ ¢

Adding coins

# Sort and Count

Remember, it's easiest to count coins when you start with the largest amount.

This is 42¢.

25 ¢   35 ¢   40 ¢   41 ¢   42 ¢

Draw the coins in order from greatest to least value. Then count them to find the total amount.

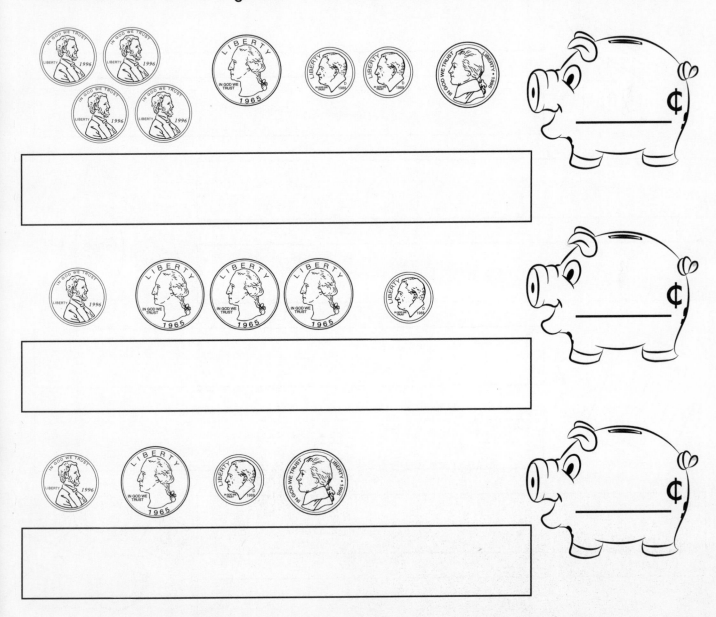

# Same Amounts with Different Coins

Think of two ways to show each amount. Draw the coins.

1.

2.

75¢

1.

2.

35¢

1.

2.

Glue
50¢

Markers
90¢

1.

2.

1.

2.

60¢

Showing amounts in two ways

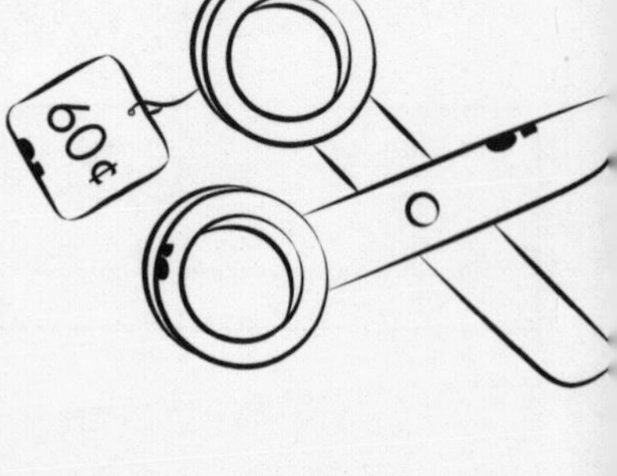

# Makes Cents

You can use the cent sign (¢) or a dollar sign ($) with a decimal point (.) to show amounts under one dollar. For example, if something costs 53 cents, you can write it as 53¢ or $0.53.

Write each price using a dollar sign and decimal point.

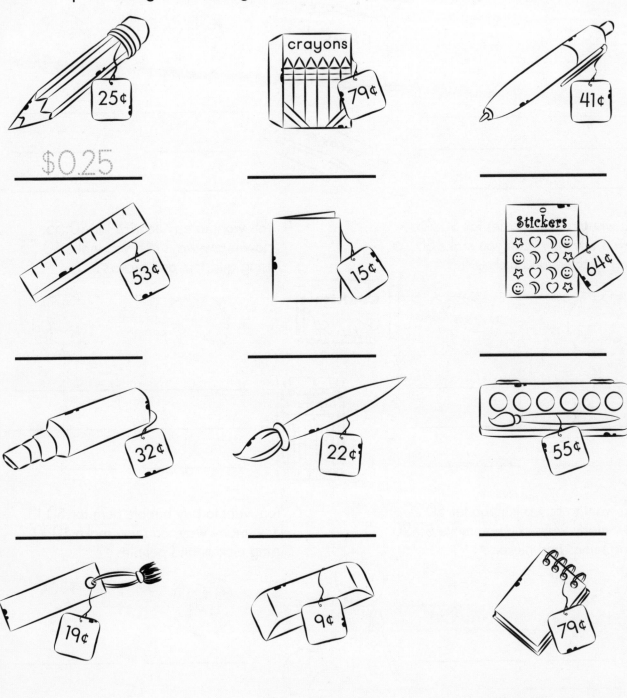

$0.25

# Money for Munchies

Solve the problems.

1. You want buy chips for $0.50.
   How many ways can you make $0.50
   using quarters and nickels?

   _____  2    _____  0

   _____       _____

   _____       _____

2. You want to buy a candy bar for $0.60.
   How many ways can you make $0.60
   using quarters and nickels?

   _____       _____

   _____       _____

   _____       _____

3. You want to buy cookies for $0.75.
   How many ways can you make $0.75
   using quarters and nickels?

   _____       _____

   _____       _____

   _____       _____

4. You want to buy licorice for $0.55.
   How many ways can you make $0.55
   using quarters and nickels?

   _____       _____

   _____       _____

   _____       _____

5. You want to buy a lollipop for $0.20.
   How many ways can you make $0.20
   using dimes and nickels?

   _____       _____

   _____       _____

   _____       _____

6. You want to buy bubble gum for $0.10.
   How many ways can you make $0.10
   using nickels and pennies?

   _____       _____

   _____       _____

   _____       _____

Showing amounts more than one way

# Making Change

Solve the problems. Show your answers.

1. Natalie has quarters and/or nickels in her pocket. She has 40¢ in all.
   What are the two possibilities?

---

---

2. Jordan has quarters and/or nickels in his pocket. He has 70¢ in all.
   What are the three possibilities?

---

---

---

3. Choose an amount between $0.50 and $0.99.  Draw the amount two ways.

   My amount is _____ .

# At the Store

Solve the problems.

| You have: | What is the total amount? | You want to buy: | Can you buy it? |
|---|---|---|---|
|  |  |  |  |
|  |  |  |  |
|  |  |  |  |

Answer the questions.

1. If you wanted to buy two jump ropes, would $5.00 be enough? _____

2. How much would three hula-hoops cost? _____

3. How much more is a yo-yo than a jump rope? _____

Solving money word problems

# Making Change

Solve the problems.

1. Ashley buys a new notebook at the store for 85¢. She pays with one dollar. How much change will she get back?

2. Joey buys a joke book for 90¢. He pays with one dollar. What will his change be?

3. Hannah buys a new gel pen for 50¢. She pays with one dollar. How much change will she get back?

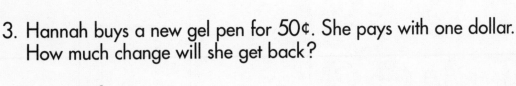

4. John buys a ruler for 35¢. He pays with one dollar. What will his change be?

5. Amy buys a clipboard for 99¢. She pays with one dollar. How much change will she get back?

6. Matthew buys a used comic book for 37¢. He pays with one dollar. What will his change be?

Comic Book

# Going Shopping

First count your money.
Then decide if you have the right amount of money to buy the item or too much.
Finally, if you have too much money, write how much change you will get back.

| Item and Price | Money in Your Pocket | What is the total amount? | Will you get change back? | How much change? |
|---|---|---|---|---|
| 🚗 50¢ | quarter, dime, dime, dime | 55¢ | yes | 5¢ |
| ⛵ 75¢ | quarter, quarter, quarter | | | |
| ✈ 70¢ | quarter, nickel, nickel, nickel, quarter, nickel, nickel | | | |
| 🚜 85¢ | quarter, quarter, quarter, dime | | | |
| 🚚 65¢ | quarter, quarter, quarter, quarter | | | |
| 🏎 90¢ | quarter, quarter, dime, dime, dime, dime | | | |

Check Out

Solving money word problems; making change

# It All Adds Up

Write the total amount using dollars and cents.

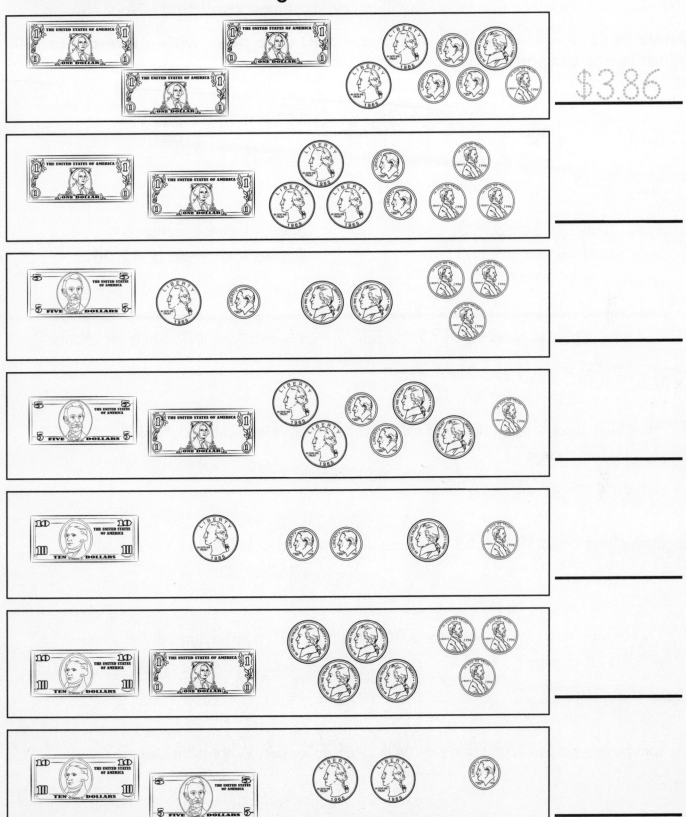

$3.86

# More Shopping

To make change, count on from the cost of the item to the amount you paid.
The difference between the cost of the item and the amount you paid is your change.

**Annie buys a new pair of mittens for $3.00. She pays with a five-dollar bill. What is her change?**

Step 1:  Count on from $3.00
         until you get to $5.00.

Step 2: Count the change.
**Annie's change is $2.00.**

---

1. Paul buys a pair of socks for $1.75. He pays with a five-dollar bill. What is his change?

2. Alice buys a set of three stockings for $4.89. She pays with a five-dollar bill.
   What is her change?

3. Elaine buys a scarf for $6.55. She pays with a ten-dollar bill. What is her change?

4. Zack buys a new pair of boots for $7.50. He pays with a ten-dollar bill.
   What is his change?

5. Tom buys a hat for $5.95. He pays with a ten-dollar bill. What is his change?

*Solving money word problems*

# Losers Weepers

1. Kaylie lost a coin. She started with $3.50, but now she only has three one-dollar bills and one quarter. What coin did she lose?

   Draw what Kaylie has now.                    Draw what coin she lost.

2. Andrew lost a coin. He started with $1.76, but now he only has one dollar bill, two quarters, and one penny. What coin did he lose?

   Draw what Andrew has now.                    Draw what coin he lost.

3. Erin lost a coin. She started with $5.25, but now she only has one five-dollar bill, one dime, and one nickel. What coin did she lose?

   Draw what Erin has now.                       Draw what coin she lost.

4. Jason lost a coin. He started with $6.91, but now he only has one five-dollar bill, one dollar bill, three quarters, one dime, and one penny. What coin did he lose?

   Draw what Jason has now.                      Draw what coin he lost.

# Summer Fun

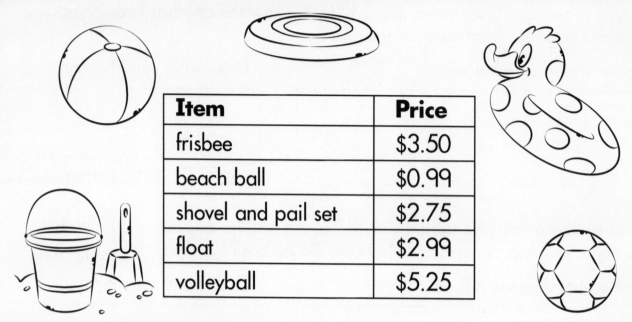

| Item | Price |
|------|-------|
| frisbee | $3.50 |
| beach ball | $0.99 |
| shovel and pail set | $2.75 |
| float | $2.99 |
| volleyball | $5.25 |

Use the chart to solve the problems.

1. You have $10.00. Estimate to see if you have enough to buy a beach ball and a volleyball.

2. Erica wants a new float to take on vacation. If she pays with a five-dollar bill, what will her change be?

3. David and his brother want to buy a new frisbee to share. They have saved $3.00 from their allowances. How much more money do they need to save before they can buy the frisbee?

4. Shelby and her cousin love to build sand castles at the beach, but their shovel broke. How much will they have to pay to buy a new one?

5. Estimate how much money it would cost to buy one of each item?

*Using a chart to solve money word problems*

# Zoo Pass Prices

| Children 2 and under | Free |
|---|---|
| Children under 12 | $10.00 |
| Adults (age 13 and up) | $15.00 |

Use the chart to solve the problems.

1. Nathan's family is thinking about getting membership passes to the zoo for everyone in the family. The family includes Nathan's 1-year-old sister, mom, dad, and himself. He is 8 years old. How much would it cost for Nathan's family buy passes?

2. The Roberts family includes two children (ages 5 and 7), Mr. and Mrs. Roberts, and Grandma Shirley. How much would they have to pay for passes to the zoo?

3. Aunt Lisa is planning to buy zoo passes for her sister and two nieces as a gift. The children are 1 and 4. How much will the zoo passes cost?

4. Jeffrey wants to use the money he got for his 9th birthday to buy a zoo pass for himself and his dad. Will $30.00 be enough for the two of them?

5. The Harts and Johnsons are buying passes so their families can go to the zoo together. Mr. and Mrs. Hart have a 6-year-old son and 2-year-old twin girls. Mr. and Mrs. Johnson have a 5-year-old son. How much will the Hart's have to pay for their passes?

   How much will the Johnson's have to pay?

   How much will the two families pay together?

# How Much to Play?

| | | | |
|---|---|---|---|
| $125.00 | | | |
| $100.00 | | ▓ | |
| $75.00 | ▓ | ▓ | |
| $50.00 | ▓ | ▓ | ▓ |
| | Soccer | Football | Baseball |

Use the graph to answer the questions.

1. Which sport is the most expensive to play? _____

2. Which is the least expensive? _____

3. How much more is it to play football than baseball? _____

4. How much would it cost to play all three sports? _____

5. You have $60.00 saved up. How much more money will you need to play soccer?

_____

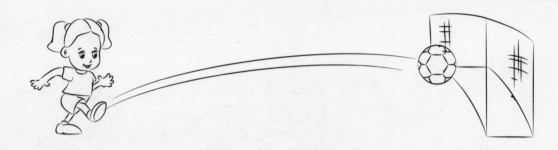

Using a graph to solve money word problems

# Time to the Hour and Half-Hour

Match the clocks that show the same time.

4:30

3:00

2:00

7:00

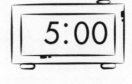
5:00

9:30

8:00

11:30

# Time to the Quarter Hour and 5-Minute Intervals

Match the clocks that show the same time.

**11:45**

**1:25**

**7:35**

**2:15**

**4:55**

**10:10**

**6:45**

**8:15**

Reviewing time to the quarter hour and 5-minute intervals

# Telling Time

Write the correct time.

_____

_____

_____

_____

_____

_____

_____

_____

_____

_____

_____

_____

# Time in Written Form

Circle the correct time.

Nine thirty
Nine forty-five

One fifteen
Two fifteen

Ten minutes after seven
Seven twenty

Five minutes after one
One twenty-five

Three fifty
Three fifty-five

Five thirty
Five forty

Four forty-five
Four fifteen

Ten after six
Six thirty

Twelve fifty-five
Eleven o'clock

Eight thirty
Eight fifty

Ten forty-five
Ten fifteen

Twelve thirty-five
Half past twelve

Recognizing time in written form

# Showing Time

Draw the hour and minute hand on each clock to show the correct time.

2:55

7:12

3:43

11:28

5:50

8:15

4:30

9:00

10:01

9:17

1:35

6:45

# How Long is a Minute?

Estimate whether each activity will take more than, less than, or about one minute. Then time yourself and record how long it takes. How well did you do with estimating?

| Activity | Estimate | Actual |
|---|---|---|
| Pouring a bowl of cereal | more than 1 minute<br>less than 1 minute<br>about 1 minute | |
| Reading a book | more than 1 minute<br>less than 1 minute<br>about 1 minute | |
| Doing your homework | more than 1 minute<br>less than 1 minute<br>about 1 minute | |

Think of other activities that you can time. See which ones take more than a minute, which ones take less than a minute, and which ones take about one minute to do. Record them on the chart below.

| More than 1 minute | Less than 1 minute | About 1 minute |
|---|---|---|
| | | |
| | | |
| | | |

Understanding the length of a minute

# Elapsed Time to the Hour and Half-Hour

Read both clocks. Write how much time has elapsed.

**START**    **STOP**      **START**    **STOP**

Elapsed Time: _____      Elapsed Time: _____

**START**    **STOP**      **START**    **STOP**

Elapsed Time: _____      Elapsed Time: _____

**START**    **STOP**      **START**    **STOP**

3:30   7:30    5:18   6:18

Elapsed Time: _____      Elapsed Time: _____

**START**    **STOP**      **START**    **STOP**

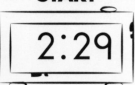 

2:29   2:59    6:36   9:36

Elapsed Time: _____      Elapsed Time: _____

# Elapsed Time to the Quarter Hour and 5-Minute Intervals

Read the elapsed time and write the new time.

| NOW | 10 MINUTES LATER | NOW | 15 MINUTES LATER |
|---|---|---|---|
|  | _____ |  | _____ |

| NOW | 15 MINUTES LATER | NOW | 5 MINUTES LATER |
|---|---|---|---|
| | _____ |  | _____ |

| NOW | 5 MINUTES LATER | NOW | 15 MINUTES LATER |
|---|---|---|---|
| | _____ | | _____ |

| NOW | 5 MINUTES LATER | NOW | 10 MINUTES LATER |
|---|---|---|---|
| | _____ | | _____ |

Understanding elapsed time: quarter hour and 5-minute intervals

# Library Programs

| Program | Begins | Ends |
|---|---|---|
| Storytime | 9:00 | 9:30 |
| Writing Workshop | 12:00 | 1:00 |
| Book Discussion | 2:00 | 3:15 |
| Puppet Show | 4:00 | 4:45 |
| Craft Class | 4:30 | 5:30 |

Use the schedule to solve the problems.

1. Clay is in the book discussion. Then he stays for the puppet show. How long is Clay at the library?

2. Beth is a member of the book discussion. She is thinking about joining the craft class, too. How much spare time would she have between the two programs?

3. Jessica gets out a school one hour before the craft class begins. What time does she get out of school?

4. Nicholas goes to the writing workshop. He wants to join the book discussion, too. How long will he have to wait between the programs?

5. Jacob goes to storytime. How long is the program?

6. Kimberly has dinner one hour after the puppet show ends. What time does she eat dinner?

Using a schedule to solve time word problems

# Using a Calendar

## JANUARY

| Sun | Mon | Tues | Wed | Thurs | Fri | Sat |
|-----|-----|------|-----|-------|-----|-----|
|     |     |      | 1   | 2     | 3   | 4   |
| 5   | 6   | 7    | 8   | 9     | 10  | 11  |
| 12  | 13  | 14   | 15  | 16    | 17  | 18  |
| 19  | 20  | 21   | 22  | 23    | 24  | 25  |
| 26  | 27  | 28   | 29  | 30    | 31  |     |

Use the calendar to answer the questions.

1. How many Wednesdays are in this month? _____

2. What day of the week is January 23? _____

3. Write the date that is five days after January 12. _____

4. What date will it be one week after January 20? _____

5. What is the last day of this month? _____

Using a calendar to solve time problems

# Reviewing Coins

Match the coins to the correct amount.

46¢

53¢

89¢

24¢

92¢

71¢

78¢

40¢

# Counting Coins

Draw the coins in order from greatest to least value.
Then count them to find the total amount.

Adding coins

# Money Problems

## Solve the problems.

1. Jessica and her brother Ian have a lemonade stand. They sell lemonade for 10¢ a glass. By the end of the first day, they sold 20 glasses. How much money did they make that first day?

   The next day, Jessica and Ian sold cookies with the lemonade. They charged 25¢ for a cookie and a glass of lemonade. They only had four customers that day because it rained all afternoon. If all the customers bought a cookie and a glass of lemonade, how much money did Jessica and Ian make?

   How much money did Jessica and Ian make altogether for both days?

   How much more money did they make the first day than the second day?

2. Lynn and her friend Natalie collected donations for the food shelter. They set up a table in Lynn's front yard and ask for canned food or money donations. At the end of the first day, Lynn and Natalie collected 20 canned food items. They also received four dollar bills, five quarters, and eight dimes. How much money did they collect?

   The second day, Lynn and Natalie decided to give a sticker to each person who donated food or money. They bought three packs of stickers for 50¢ per pack. How much money did Lynn and Natalie spend on stickers?

   During the second day, Lynn and Natalie collected 30 canned food items. They also received five dollar bills, ten quarters, three nickels, and two pennies. How much money did they collect?

   How much money did Lynn and Natalie collect altogether on both days?

   Subtract the cost of the stickers from the total amount of money they received to figure out how much money Lynn and Natalie donated to the food shelter.

# Earning Money

| Chore | Money Earned |
|---|---|
| make bed | 50¢ |
| feed pets | $1.25 |
| take out trash | 75¢ |
| plant flowers | $2.00 |
| vacuum | $1.00 |
| wash dishes | $1.50 |

We have to work to earn money to buy the things that we want and need.

Use the chart to answer the questions.

1.  Which job allows you to earn the most money in one day?


2.  You want to buy a new kite for $3.00. How many times will you have to make your bed to earn the money?


    How many times would you have to take out the trash to earn $3.00?


3.  If you feed your pets for the whole week, including the weekend, would you have enough money to buy a new book for $6.99? Explain.


4.  How much would you earn if you did all the jobs one time?


5.  If you make your bed everyday for two weeks, how much money would you earn?

Using a chart to solve money word problems

# Answer Key

Please take time to review the work your child has completed and remember to praise both success and effort. If your child makes a mistake, let him or her know that mistakes are a part of learning. Then explain the correct answer and how to find it. Taking the time to help your child and an active interest in his or her progress shows that you feel learning is important.

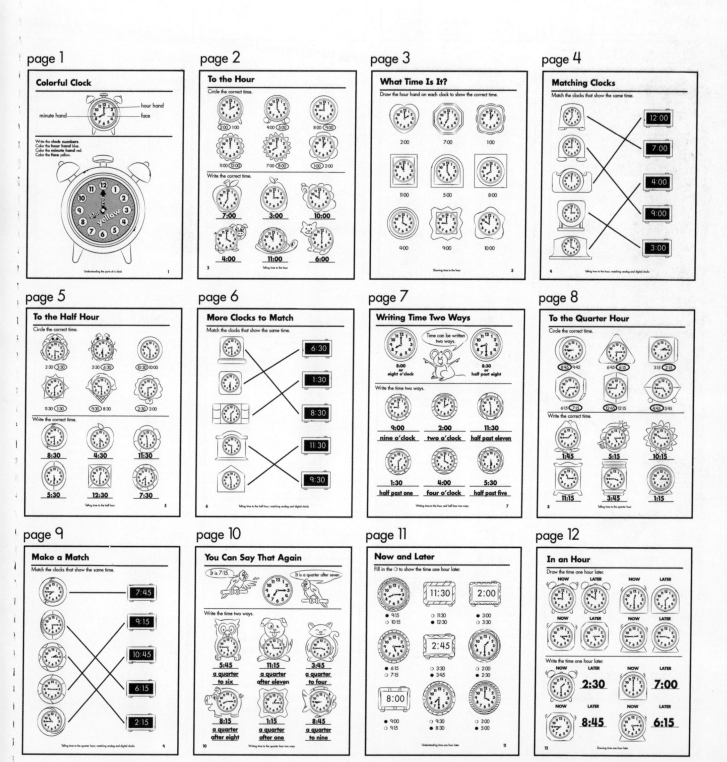

## page 13

**Five at a Time**

There are 60 minutes in an hour.
Each number on a clock represents 5 minutes.

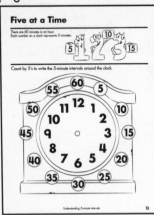

Count by 5's to write the 5-minute intervals around the clock.

Clock with numbers: 55, 60, 5, 50, 45, 40, 35, 30, 25, 20, 15, 10

*Understanding 5-minute intervals*                    13

## page 14

**Time for Fives**

Circle the correct time.

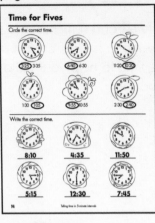

3:25  3:35    6:40  6:30    11:20  10:20

1:30  1:05    4:55  10:55    2:30  2:40

Write the correct time.

8:10     4:35     11:50

5:15     12:30     7:45

14                    *Telling time in 5-minute intervals*

## page 15

**Watch the Time**

Match the clocks that show the same time.

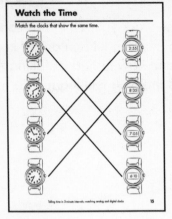

2:55

8:35

7:05

6:10

*Telling time in 5-minute intervals; matching analog and digital clocks*    15

## page 16

**Same Time**

Match each clock with the correct time.

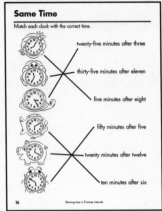

twenty-five minutes after three

thirty-five minutes after eleven

five minutes after eight

fifty minutes after five

twenty minutes after twelve

ten minutes after six

16                    *Showing time in 5-minute intervals*

## page 17

**One at a Time**

Each hour is made up of 60 minutes.
The 60 minutes go around a clock.

Count by 1's to write the minutes around the clock.

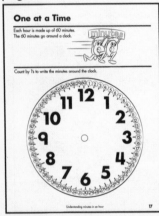

*Understanding minutes in an hour*                    17

## page 18

**To the Minute**

Circle the correct time.

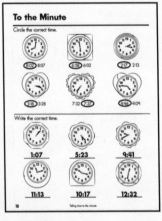

8:02  8:07    6:58  6:02    2:17  2:13

3:18  3:28    7:32  7:37    4:46  4:09

Write the correct time.

1:07     5:23     9:41

11:13     10:17     12:32

18                    *Telling time to the minute*

## page 19

**Minute Match**

Match the clocks that show the same time.

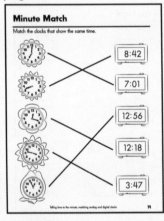

8:42

7:01

12:56

12:18

3:47

*Telling time to the minute; matching analog and digital clocks*    19

## page 20

**One to One**

Match each clock with the correct time.

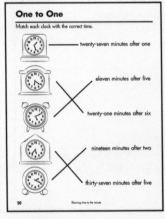

twenty-seven minutes after one

eleven minutes after five

twenty-one minutes after six

nineteen minutes after two

thirty-seven minutes after five

20                    *Showing time to the minute*

## page 21

**Do You Have the Time?**

Draw the hour hand on each clock to show the correct time.

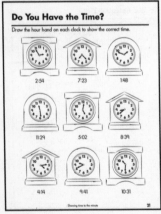

2:54     7:23     1:48

11:29     5:02     8:39

4:14     9:41     10:31

22                    *Showing time to the minute*    21

## page 22

**Got a Minute?**

How many times can you do each activity in a minute? First estimate. Then do the activity and record the actual number.

How many times can you stomp your feet in 1 minute?
Estimate _____
Actual **Answers will vary.**

How many times can you say,
"Lucy left her lollipop in the lunch line" in 1 minute?
Estimate _____
Actual **Answers will vary.**

How many jumping jacks can you do in 1 minute?
Estimate _____
Actual **Answers will vary.**

How many times can you write your first and last name in 1 minute?
Estimate _____
Actual **Answers will vary.**

How many times can you snap your fingers in 1 minute?
Estimate _____
Actual **Answers will vary.**

22                    *Understanding the length of a minute*

## page 23

**Passing Time**

Elapsed time is used to find out how much time has passed. If you start playing a game at 3:00 and finish at 3:30, the elapsed time is 30 minutes or a half hour.

Read both clocks. Write how much time has elapsed.

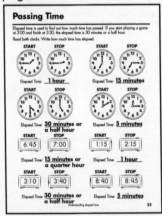

START  STOP       START  STOP
Elapsed Time: **1 hour**    Elapsed Time: **15 minutes**

START  STOP       START  STOP
Elapsed Time: **30 minutes or a half hour**    Elapsed Time: **5 minutes**

START  STOP       START  STOP
6:45  7:00    1:15  2:15
Elapsed Time: **15 minutes or a quarter hour**    Elapsed Time: **1 hour**

START  STOP       START  STOP
3:10  3:40    8:40  8:45
Elapsed Time: **30 minutes or a half hour**    Elapsed Time: **5 minutes**

*Understanding elapsed time*    23

## page 24

**How Much Time Elapsed?**

Read each problem and solve.

Lisa's bus picked her up at 8:00. She got to school at 8:15. How long was she on the bus?
start time **8:00**
finish time **8:15**
elapsed time **15 minutes or a quarter hour**

Mary's math class started at 10:30 and ended at 11:15. How long was the class?
start time **10:30**
finish time **11:15**
elapsed time **45 minutes**

Tommy went to lunch at 12:00 and then to recess at 12:30. How long was lunchtime?
start time **12:00**
finish time **12:30**
elapsed time **30 minutes or a half hour**

Fred started writing a story at 2:00 and finished at 2:25. How long did it take him to write his story?
start time **2:00**
finish time **2:25**
elapsed time **25 minutes**

Aaron had a snack after school at 4:10. He started his homework 15 minutes later. What time did Aaron start his homework?
start time **4:10**
finish time **15 minutes**
elapsed time **4:25**

Rosemary and her mom went to the store at 6:00. They were gone for one hour. What time did they get home?
start time **6:00**
finish time **1 hour**
elapsed time **7:00**

Curtis practiced the piano at 7:30. He practiced three songs in twenty minutes. What time did Curtis finish practicing?
start time **7:30**
finish time **20 minutes**
elapsed time **7:50**

Laura likes to read before she goes to sleep. She started reading at 8:00 and read for 30 minutes. What time did Laura stop reading?
start time **8:00**
finish time **30 minutes**
elapsed time **8:30**

24                    *Solving word problems with elapsed time*

## page 25

**Practice Sessions**

| Sport | Begins | Ends |
|---|---|---|
| Baseball | 6:00 | 8:00 |
| Football | 4:30 | 5:30 |
| Swimming | 5:15 | 6:15 |
| Soccer | 4:00 | 6:00 |

Use the schedule to answer the questions.

1. Which practice begins at a quarter after five? **swimming**
2. How long does the baseball practice last? **2 hours**
3. Which practice starts 30 minutes after soccer? **football**
4. Which practices are two hours long? **baseball and soccer**
5. Which practice ends the latest? **baseball**

*Using a schedule to solve time problems*    25

## page 26

**Things To Do**

| | visit grandparents | go to grocery store | get haircut |
|---|---|---|---|
| 2 hours | | | |
| 1 hour and 30 minutes | | | |
| 1 hour | | | |
| 30 minutes | | | |

Use the graph to answer the questions.

1. Which activity will take the least amount of time?
**haircut**
2. Which will take the most amount of time?
**visit grandparents**
3. How much longer is the trip to the grocery store than getting a haircut?
**1 hour**
4. How long will it take to do all three activities?
**4 hours**
5. Name another activity that takes about the same amount of time as getting your haircut.
**Answers will vary.**

26                    *Using a graph to solve time problems*

## page 27

**Calendar Time**

**JUNE**

| Sun | Mon | Tues | Wed | Thurs | Fri | Sat |
|---|---|---|---|---|---|---|
| 1 | 2 | 3 | 4 | 5 | 6 | 7 |
| 8 | 9 | 10 | 11 | 12 | 13 | 14 |
| 15 | 16 | 17 | 18 | 19 | 20 | 21 |
| 22 | 23 | 24 | 25 | 26 | 27 | 28 |
| 29 | 30 | | | | | |

Use the calendar to answer the questions.

1. What is the first day of the week? **Sunday**
2. How many days are in one week? **7 days**
3. How many Mondays are in this month? **5**
4. What day of the week is June 27? **Friday**
5. Write the date that is five days after June 6. **June 11**
6. What date will it be one week after June 19? **June 26**
7. What is the last day of this month? **Monday**

*Using a calendar to solve time problems*    27

## page 28

**Coins**

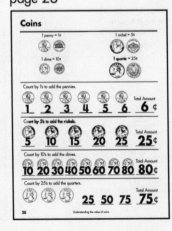

1 penny = 1¢                    1 nickel = 5¢
1 dime = 10¢                    1 quarter = 25¢

Count by 1's to add the pennies.
1  2  3  4  5  6    Total Amount **6¢**

Count by 5's to add the nickels.
5  10  15  20  25    Total Amount **25¢**

Count by 10's to add the dimes.
10 20 30 40 50 60 70 80    Total Amount **80¢**

Count by 25's to add the quarters.
25  50  75    Total Amount **75¢**

28                    *Understanding the value of coins*

### Coin Match
Match the coins to the correct amount.

35¢
42¢
78¢
13¢
81¢
94¢
39¢
67¢

### More or Less?
Count the coins. Then write >, <, or = to compare the amounts.

▷
◁
▷
◁

Write >, <, or = to compare the amounts.

| 74¢ > 47¢ | 91¢ > 61¢ | 25¢ = 25¢ | 41¢ > 14¢ |
| 19¢ < 29¢ | 20¢ < 70¢ | 31¢ > 13¢ | 51¢ = 51¢ |
| 21¢ < 12¢ | 83¢ < 88¢ | 69¢ = 96¢ | 53¢ > 53¢ |
| 34¢ < 40¢ | 70¢ > 17¢ | 94¢ = 49¢ | 11¢ > 11¢ |

### Counting Coins
Count the coins. Write the total amount.

Total **68** ¢

Total **56** ¢

Total **96** ¢

Total **67** ¢

Total **74** ¢

### Counting Big to Small
Counting money is easiest when you start with the largest amount.

First count the quarters.   **25** ¢
   **50** ¢

Next add the dimes.   **60** ¢
   **70** ¢
   **80** ¢
   **90** ¢

Then add the nickels.   **95** ¢

Finally add the pennies.   **96** ¢
   **97** ¢
   **98** ¢
   **99** ¢

### Sort and Count
Remember, it's easiest to count coins when you start with the largest amount.

This is 42¢.

**25¢  35¢  40¢  41¢  42¢**

Draw the coins in order from greatest to least value. Then count them to find the total amount.

(25)(10)(10)(5)(5)(1)(1)(1)   **59** ¢

(25)(10)(10)(5)(1)   **86** ¢

(25)(25)(25)(10)(1)   **41** ¢

(25)(10)(5)(1)

### Same Amounts with Different Coins
Think of two ways to show each amount. Draw the coins.

1. (25)(25)(25)
2. (25)(25)(10)(10)(5)

1. (25)(10)
2. (10)(10)(10)(10)

1. (10)(10)
2. (25)(25)(5)(5)(5)(5)(5)

1. (25)(25)(10)(5)
2. (10)(10)(10)(10)(10)

1. (25)(25)(10)
2. (25)(10)(10)(10)(5)

### Makes Cents
You can use the cent sign (¢) or a dollar sign ($) with a decimal point (.) to show amounts under one dollar. For example, if something costs 53 cents, you can write it as 53¢ or $0.53.

Write each price using a dollar sign and decimal point.

**$0.25**   **$0.79**   **$0.41**

**$0.53**   **$0.15**   **$0.64**

**$0.32**   **$0.22**   **$0.55**

**$0.19**   **$0.09**   **$0.79**

### Money for Munchies
Solve the problems.

1. You want buy chips for $0.50. How many ways can you make $0.50 using quarters and nickels?

2 1 0
1 3 5
0 10 10

2. You want to buy a candy bar for $0.60. How many ways can you make $0.60 using quarters and nickels?

2 2 1
1 5 7
0 2 12

3. You want to buy cookies for $0.75. How many ways can you make $0.75 using quarters and nickels?

3 2 1 0
0 5 10 15
0 5 6 11

4. You want to buy licorice for $0.55. How many ways can you make $0.55 using quarters and nickels?

2 1 0
1 6 11

5. You want to buy a lollipop for $0.20. How many ways can you make $0.20 using dimes and nickels?

2 1 0
0 2 4

6. You want to buy bubble gum for $0.10. How many ways can you make $0.10 using nickels and pennies?

2 1 0
0 5 10

### Making Change
Solve the problems. Show your answers.

1. Natalia has quarters and/or nickels in her pocket. She has 40¢ in all. What are the two possibilities?

(25)(5)(5)(5)
(5)(5)(5)(5)(5)(5)(5)(5)

2. Jordan has quarters and/or nickels in his pocket. He has 70¢ in all. What are the three possibilities?

(25)(25)(5)(5)(5)(5)
(25)(5)(5)(5)(5)(5)(5)(5)(5)
(5)(5)(5)(5)(5)(5)(5)(5)(5)(5)(5)(5)(5)(5)

3. Choose an amount between $0.50 and $0.99. Draw the amount two ways.

My amount is **Answers** will vary.

### At the Store
Solve the problems.

| You have: | What is the total amount? | You want to buy: | Can you buy it? |
|---|---|---|---|
| | **$1.20** | | **NO** |
| | **$2.15** | | **NO** |
| | **$2.00** | | **YES** |

Answer the questions.

1. If you wanted to buy two jump ropes, would $5.00 be enough? **YES**

2. How much would three hula-hoops cost? **$6.00**

3. How much more is a yo-yo than a jump rope? **$0.75**

### Making Change
Solve the problems.

1. Ashley buys a new notebook at the store for 85¢. She pays with one dollar. How much change will she get back?   **$0.15**

2. Joey buys a joke book for 90¢. He pays with one dollar. What will his change be?   **$0.10**

3. Hannah buys a new gel pen for 50¢. She pays with one dollar. How much change will she get back?   **$0.50**

4. John buys a ruler for 35¢. He pays with one dollar. What will his change be?   **$0.65**

5. Amy buys a clipboard for 99¢. She pays with one dollar. How much change will she get back?   **$0.01**

6. Mathew buys a used comic book for 37¢. He pays with one dollar. What will his change be?   **$0.63**

### Going Shopping
First count your money.
Then decide if you have the right amount of money to buy the item or too much.
Finally, if you have too much money, write how much change you will get back.

| Item and Price | Money in Your Pocket | What is the total amount? | Will you get change back? | How much change? |
|---|---|---|---|---|
| | | 55¢ | YES | 5¢ |
| | | 75¢ | NO | – |
| | | 75¢ | YES | 10¢ |
| | | 85¢ | NO | – |
| | | $1.00 | YES | 10¢ |
| | | 90¢ | YES | 20¢ |

### It All Adds Up
Write the total amount using dollars and cents.

**$3.86**

**$2.99**

**$5.48**

**$6.81**

**$10.51**

**$11.23**

**$15.60**

### More Shopping
To make change, count on from the cost of the item to the amount you paid. The difference between the cost of the item and the amount you paid is your change.

Annie buys a new pair of mittens for $3.00. She pays with a five-dollar bill. What is her change?

 + + =

Step 1: Count on from $3.00 until you get to $5.00.

Step 2: Count the change. **Annie's change is $2.00.**

1. Paul buys a pair of socks for $1.75. He pays with a five-dollar bill. What is his change?
**$3.25**

2. Alice buys a set of three stockings for $4.89. She pays with a five-dollar bill. What is her change?
**$0.11**

3. Elaine buys a scarf for $6.55. She pays with a ten-dollar bill. What is her change?
**$3.45**

4. Zack buys a new pair of boots for $7.50. She pays with a ten-dollar bill. What is her change?
**$2.50**

5. Tom buys a hat for $5.95. He pays with a ten-dollar bill. What is his change?
**$4.05**

### Losers Weepers
1. Kaylie lost a coin. She started with $3.50, but now she only has three one-dollar bills and one quarter. What coin did she lose?

Draw what Kaylie has now.
1 1 1 (25)

Draw what coin she lost.
(25)

2. Andrew lost a coin. He started with $1.76, but now he only has one dollar bill, two quarters, and one penny. What coin did he lose?

1 (25)(25)(1)

(25)

3. Erin lost a coin. She started with $5.25, but now she only has one five-dollar bill, one dime, and one nickel. What coin did she lose?

Draw what Erin has now.
5 (10)(5)

Draw what coin she lost.
(10)

4. Jason lost a coin. He started with $6.91, but now he only has one five-dollar bill, one dollar bill, three quarters, one dime, and one penny. What coin did he lose?

Draw what Jason has now.
5 1 (25)(25)(25)(10)(1)

Draw what coin he lost.
(5)

### Summer Fun

| Item | Price |
|---|---|
| frisbee | $3.50 |
| beach ball | $0.99 |
| shovel and pail set | $2.75 |
| float | $2.99 |
| volleyball | $5.25 |

Use the chart to solve the problems.

1. You have $10.00. Estimate to see if you have enough to buy a beach ball and a volleyball.
**Yes. It would cost about $6.25.**

2. Erica wants a new float to take on vacation. If she pays with a five-dollar bill, what will her change be?
**$2.01**

3. David and his brother want to buy a new frisbee to share. They have saved $3.00 from their allowances. How much more money do they need to save before they can buy the frisbee?
**$0.50**

4. Shelby and her cousin love to build sand castles at the beach, but their shovel broke. How much will they have to pay to buy a new one?
**$2.75**

5. Estimate how much it would cost to buy one of each item?
**$15.50**

Answers   **63**

## Zoo Pass Prices

| Children 2 and under | Free |
|---|---|
| Children under 12 | $10.00 |
| Adults (age 13 and up) | $15.00 |

Use the chart to solve the problems.

1. Nathan's family is thinking about getting membership passes to the zoo for everyone in the family. The family includes Nathan's 1-year-old sister, mom, dad, and himself. He is 8 years old. How much would it cost for Nathan's family buy passes? **$40.00.**

2. The Roberts family includes two children (ages 5 and 7), Mr. and Mrs. Roberts, and Grandma Shirley. How much would they have to pay for passes to the zoo? **$65.00**

3. Aunt Lisa is planning to buy zoo passes for her sister and two nieces as a gift. The children are 1 and 4. How much will the zoo passes cost? **$25.00**

4. Jeffrey wants to use the money he got for his 9th birthday to buy a zoo pass for himself and his dad. Will $30.00 be enough for the two of them? **Yes. The passes will cost $25.00**

5. The Harts and Johnsons are buying passes so their families can go to the zoo together. Mr. and Mrs. Hart have a 6-year-old son and 2-year-old twin girls. Mr. and Mrs. Johnson have a 5-year-old son. How much will the Harts have to pay for their passes? **$40.00**

How much will the Johnson's have to pay? **$40.00**

How much will the two families pay together? **$80.00**

## How Much to Play?

Use the graph to answer the questions.

1. Which sport is the most expensive to play? **football**

2. Which is the least expensive? **baseball**

3. How much more is it to play football than baseball? **$50.00**

4. How much would it cost to play all three sports? **$225.00**

5. You have $60.00 saved up. How much more money will you need to play soccer? **$15.00**

## Time to the Hour and Half-Hour

Match the clocks that show the same time.

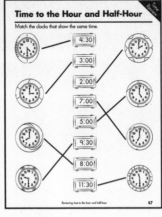

4:30
3:00
2:00
7:00
5:00
9:30
8:00
11:30

## Time to the Quarter Hour and 5-Minute Intervals

Match the clocks that show the same time.

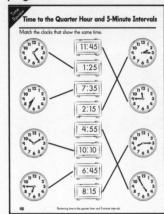

11:45
1:25
7:35
2:15
4:55
10:10
6:45
8:15

## Telling Time

Write the correct time.

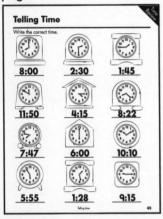

8:00    2:30    1:45
11:50    4:15    8:22
7:47    6:00    10:10
5:55    1:28    9:15

## Time in Written Form

Circle the correct time.

Nine thirty / Nine forty-five
One fifteen / Two fifteen
Ten minutes after seven / Seven twenty
Five minutes after one / One twenty-five
Three fifty / Three fifty-five
Five thirty / Five forty
Four forty-five / Four fifteen
Ten after six / Six thirty
Twelve fifty-five / Eleven o'clock
Eight thirty / Eight fifty
Ten forty-five / Ten fifteen
Twelve thirty-five / Half past twelve

## Showing Time

Draw the hour and minute hand on each clock to show the correct time.

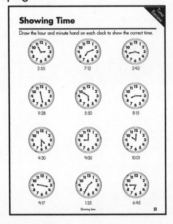

2:55    7:12    3:43
11:28    5:50    8:15
4:30    9:00    10:01
9:17    1:35    6:45

## How Long is a Minute?

Estimate whether each activity will take more than, less than, or about one minute. Then time yourself and record how long it takes. How well did you do with estimating? **Answers will vary.**

| Activity | Estimate | Actual |
|---|---|---|
| Pouring a bowl of cereal | more than 1 minute / less than 1 minute / about 1 minute | |
| Reading a book | more than 1 minute / less than 1 minute / about 1 minute | |
| Doing your homework | more than 1 minute / less than 1 minute / about 1 minute | |

Think of other activities that you can time. See which ones take more than a minute, which ones take less than a minute, and which ones take about one minute to do. Record them on the chart below.

| More than 1 minute | Less than 1 minute | About 1 minute |
|---|---|---|
| | | |
| | | |

## Elapsed Time to the Hour and Half-Hour

Read both clocks. Write how much time has elapsed.

Elapsed Time: **30 minutes or a half hour**
Elapsed Time: **2 hours**
Elapsed Time: **3 hours**
Elapsed Time: **30 minutes or a half hour**

START 3:30  STOP 7:30
Elapsed Time: **4 hours**

START 5:18  STOP 6:18
Elapsed Time: **1 hour**

START 2:29  STOP 2:59
Elapsed Time: **30 minutes or a half hour**

START 6:36  STOP 9:36
Elapsed Time: **3 hours**

## Elapsed Time to the Quarter Hour and 5-Minute Intervals

Read the elapsed time and write the new time.

NOW  10 MINUTES LATER  **3:30**
NOW  15 MINUTES LATER  **4:45**
NOW  15 MINUTES LATER  **2:30**
NOW  5 MINUTES LATER  **8:30**
NOW  5 MINUTES LATER  **11:05**
NOW  15 MINUTES LATER  **10:00**
NOW  5 MINUTES LATER  **1:15**
NOW  10 MINUTES LATER  **6:35**

## Library Programs

| Program | Begins | Ends |
|---|---|---|
| Storytime | 9:00 | 9:30 |
| Writing Workshop | 12:00 | 1:00 |
| Book Discussion | 2:00 | 3:15 |
| Puppet Show | 4:00 | 4:45 |
| Craft Class | 4:30 | 5:30 |

Use the schedule to solve the problems.

1. Clay is in the book discussion. Then he stays for the puppet show. How long is Clay at the library? **2 hours and 45 minutes**

2. Beth is a member of the book discussion. She is thinking about joining the craft class, too. How much spare time would she have between the two programs? **1 hours and 15 minutes**

3. Jessica gets out at school one hour before the craft class begins. What time does she get out of school? **3:30**

4. Nicholas goes to the writing workshop. He wants to join the book discussion, too. How long will he have to wait between the programs? **1 hour**

5. Jacob goes to storytime. How long is the program? **30 minutes or a half hour**

6. Kimberly has dinner one hour after the puppet show ends. What time does she eat dinner? **5:45**

## Using a Calendar

| | | | JANUARY | | | |
|---|---|---|---|---|---|---|
| Sun | Mon | Tues | Wed | Thurs | Fri | Sat |
| | | | 1 | 2 | 3 | 4 |
| 5 | 6 | 7 | 8 | 9 | 10 | 11 |
| 12 | 13 | 14 | 15 | 16 | 17 | 18 |
| 19 | 20 | 21 | 22 | 23 | 24 | 25 |
| 26 | 27 | 28 | 29 | 30 | 31 | |

Use the calendar to answer the questions.

1. How many Wednesdays are in this month? **5**

2. What day of the week is January 23? **Thursday**

3. Write the date that is five days after January 12. **January 17**

4. What date will it be one week after January 20? **January 27**

5. What is the last day of this month? **Friday**

## Reviewing Coins

Match the coins to the correct amount.

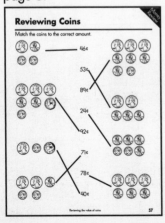

— 46¢
53¢
89¢
24¢
92¢
71¢
78¢
40¢

## Counting Coins

Draw the coins in order from greatest to least value. Then count them to find the total amount.

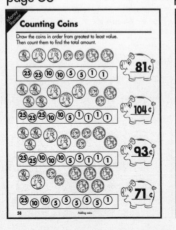

**81¢**
**104¢**
**93¢**
**71¢**

## Money Problems

Solve the problems.

1. Jessica and her brother Ian have a lemonade stand. They sell lemonade for 10¢ a glass. By the end of the first day, they sold 20 glasses. How much money did they make that first day? **$2.00**

The next day, Jessica and Ian sold cookies with the lemonade. They charged 25¢ for a cookie and a glass of lemonade. They only had four customers that day because it rained all afternoon. If all the customers bought a cookie and a glass of lemonade, how much money did Jessica and Ian make? **$1.00**

How much money did Jessica and Ian make altogether for both days? **$3.00**

How much more money did they make the first day than the second day? **$1.00**

2. Lynn and her friend Natalie collected donations for the food shelter. They set up a table in Lynn's front yard and ask for canned food or money donations. At the end of the first day, Lynn and Natalie collected 20 canned food items. They also received four dollar bills, five quarters, and eight dimes. How much money did they collect? **$6.05**

The second day, Lynn and Natalie decided to give a sticker to each person who donated food or money. They bought three packs of stickers for 50¢ per pack. How much money did Lynn and Natalie spend on stickers? **$1.50**

During the second day, Lynn and Natalie collected 30 canned food items. They also received five dollar bills, ten quarters, three nickels, and two pennies. How much money did they collect? **$7.67**

How much money did Lynn and Natalie collect altogether on both days? **$13.72**

Subtract the cost of the stickers from the total amount of money they received to figure out how much money Lynn and Natalie donated to the food shelter. **$12.22**

## Earning Money

| Chore | Money Earned |
|---|---|
| make bed | 50¢ |
| feed pets | $1.25 |
| take out trash | 75¢ |
| plant flowers | $2.00 |
| vacuum | $1.00 |
| wash dishes | $1.50 |

We have to work to earn money to buy the things that we want and need. Use the chart to answer the questions.

1. Which job allows you to earn the most money in one day? **planting flowers**

2. You want to buy a new kite for $3.00. How many times will you have to make your bed to earn the money? **6 times**

How many times would you have to take out the trash to earn $3.00? **4 times**

3. If you feed your pets for the whole week, including the weekend, would you have enough money to buy a new book for $6.99? Explain. **Yes. You would have $8.75.**

4. How much would you earn if you did all the jobs one time? **$7.00**

5. If you make your bed everyday for two weeks, how much money would you earn? **$7.00**